P9-CFX-983

Tierra del Fuego

By Peter Lourie

Amazon
Hudson River
Yukon River
Everglades
Erie Canal
Rio Grande
Mississippi River
On the Trail of Sacagawea
On the Trail of Lewis and Clark
Lost Treasure of the Inca
The Mystery of the Maya
The Lost Treasure of Captain Kidd

For older readers:

Sweat of the Sun, Tears of the Moon
River of Mountains

Tierra del Fuego

A Journey to the End of the Earth

PETER LOURIE

Boyds Mills Press

LIBRARY
FRANKLIN PIERCE COLLEGE
RINDGE, NH 03461

To Pappy and Jasmine
—P. L.

Text and photographs copyright © 2002 by Peter Lourie
All rights reserved

Published by Boyds Mills Press, Inc.
A Highlights Company
815 Church Street
Honesdale, Pennsylvania 18431
Printed in China
Visit our website at www.boydsmillspress.com

A special thank you to Oscar Pablo Zanola, the director of El Museo del Fin del Mundo in Ushuaia, Argentina

Publisher Cataloging-in-Publication Data

Lourie, Peter.
    Tierra del fuego : a journey to the end of the earth / by Peter Lourie. —1st ed.
[48] p. : col. photos., maps ;   cm.
Includes index.
Summary: A photo essay of a journey to the islands off the southern tip
of South America.
ISBN 1-56397-973-X
1. Tierra del Fuego (Argentina and Chile)—Juvenile literature.
1. Tierra del Fuego (Argentina and Chile.) I. Title.
918.276 21   CIP   F2986.L68 2002
2001096395

First edition, 2002
The text of this book is set in 13-point Goudy.

10 9 8 7 6 5 4 3 2 1

Additional photographs courtesy of:
The Library of Congress: pp. 11 (left), 25 (left)
Bedford Whaling Museum, Bedford, Massachusetts: pp. 16 (bottom), 17, 18 (top), 19
Matthew Cull: p. 35 (top)
El Museo del Fin del Mundo, Ushuaia, Argentina: pp. 11 (right), 12–15, 23–25
  (right), 26–27, 32 (right), 38 (left), 46

CONTENTS

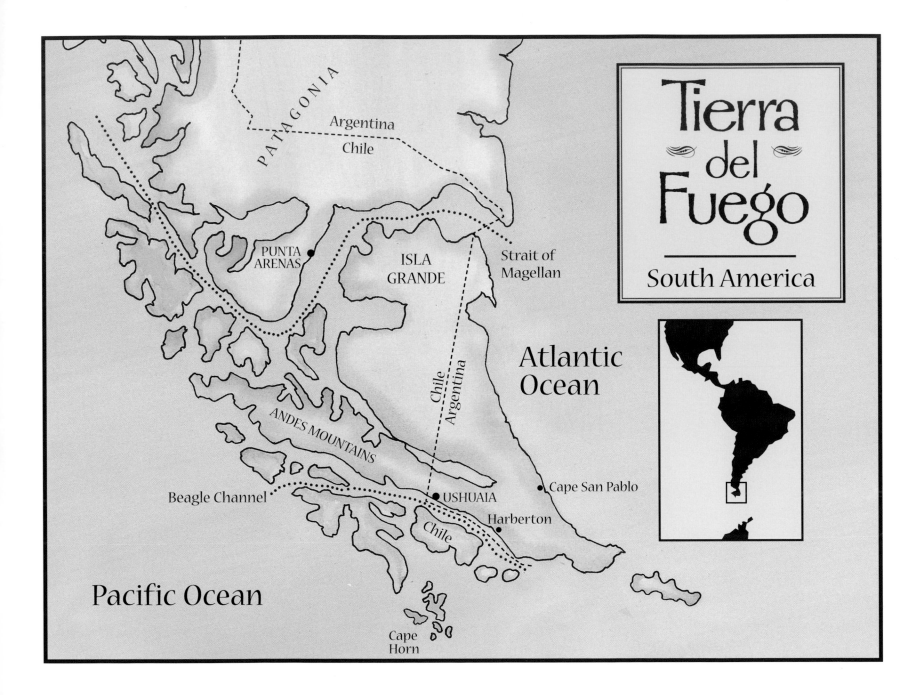

Tierra del Fuego
South America

Pacific Ocean

Atlantic Ocean

PATAGONIA

Argentina
Chile

Punta Arenas

ISLA GRANDE

Strait of Magellan

Chile
Argentina

Andes Mountains

Beagle Channel

Ushuaia

Cape San Pablo

Harberton

Chile

Cape Horn

Prologue

In 1520 Ferdinand Magellan first spotted the large island of Tierra del Fuego at the southern tip of South America. Along the island's shore, in what is now called the Strait of Magellan, he saw smoke from native fires. He never met the tribe of people who lived here, but their fires inspired him to name the island Tierra del Fuego (tee-ayŕ-rah del foo-aý-go), which is Spanish for Land of Fire.

The native people remained a mystery to explorers for another three hundred years. The land, the climate, and the waters of Tierra del Fuego were a mystery, too. For centuries after Magellan's visit, this southernmost part of Patagonia was feared by sailors for its contrary currents, powerful winds, and big waves. Cape Horn, the very tip of the southern hemisphere, is only 700 miles from the continent of Antarctica. Those seven hundred miles of water are among the roughest seas on the globe. Cape Horn and the shores around Tierra del Fuego are littered with the remains of sunken ships that for centuries have foundered in violent weather.

The Land of Fire seemed like the ultimate place to visit, a land that inspires a mixture of fear and fascination. Since I was a child, I have been fascinated by the adventures of Magellan and other explorers, by their tales of hardship and discovery at the uttermost part of the earth. It had been my dream to see with my own eyes that misty land of penguins and wild seas.

So one January, which is summer in the southern hemisphere, I decided to pursue my dream. I left the snows of Vermont behind and flew 7,000 miles south to Punta Arenas, Chile. My plan was to begin my journey through the Land of Fire on the Strait of Magellan, which forms the northern border of the big island of Tierra del Fuego, known also as Isla Grande. Then I would head south to Ushuaia (oosh-whý-ah), Argentina, the southernmost town on the earth. Ushuaia sits on the Beagle Channel, which forms the southern border of the big island. I would take my mountain bike to explore areas unreachable by car.

When I boarded the plane in Boston, the bottom of the world seemed very, very far away.

ONE

Punta Arenas, Chile

As the plane banked for a landing in Punta Arenas, the water below looked blue-black. Whitecaps glowed under a low gray sky. The atmosphere was brooding and ominous, exactly as I had imagined it.

I found a room in a hotel that overlooked the city. From my window, I gazed at the huge expanse of the Strait of Magellan and tried to picture Magellan sailing for the first time through the 350-mile pass from the Atlantic to the South Pacific.

The next morning I was anxious to explore the city. I began to assemble my mountain bike from its big traveling box. After an hour's work, the bike was ready. I grabbed my camera and

A fisherman displays his catch on the docks of Punta Arenas.

headed off through the streets of Punta Arenas (pooń-tah ah-raý-nahs), which was not at all the frontier town I had imagined. I was surprised to find a modern city of 150,000 people, with hotels and restaurants and tourists who, like me, had come to see this land of myth.

I rode down to the port, where the wind was gusting so hard out of the west that it almost blew me into the water. Fishing boats crowded the harbor. Fishermen from one boat were offloading *merluza*, a long, sharp-toothed pinkish fish, packed in boxes of ice. I watched them load more than a hundred boxes of the big fish onto a truck.

These hardworking men said that tonight they would have a party. They had been out on the water for a week and would not sail again for another month. They had been fishing up the strait, twenty hours from Punta Arenas. I figured that would have put them almost into open ocean, the South Pacific.

Magellan

In 1492, only a few years before Magellan's voyage, Christopher Columbus had crossed the Atlantic and discovered the continent of America. He was searching for a trade route from Europe to the fabulous riches of the East Indies. In those days, spices from the South Pacific, such as cinnamon, nutmeg, and ginger, were more valuable than gold. Columbus failed to find a route to Asia, but he was followed by other sailors who crossed the Atlantic to explore the coast of what is now Brazil.

Dangerous shoals and rocks around Tierra del Fuego have caused many ships to go under.

Ferdinand Magellan: The first European to see "the land of fire."

Farther and farther south the explorers traveled, in search of a passage from the Atlantic Ocean to the Pacific.

Captain Ferdinand Magellan left Seville, Spain, in 1519 in a bold attempt to circumnavigate the globe. Although he was Portugese by birth, Magellan was sailing for the king of Spain. His goal was to reach the Pacific Ocean not by rounding the tip of Africa, but by sailing west from the Atlantic Ocean through a hidden passage that he hoped to find.

After nearly a year of exploring the southern coast of South America, Magellan and his men spent a bleak winter in a wind-tossed, dead land. Rough seas and harsh weather made navigation impossible, so they set up camp near the shore. They endured many hardships. Magellan even fought off a mutiny.

One member of the crew, Antonio Pigafetta, kept a journal of these experiences. Much of what we know about Magellan's

11

A map of the New World, 1601.

voyage comes from Pigafetta, who was the official chronicler of the voyage. He records that one morning there appeared a very tall and strange figure with a face "painted red with yellow rings around his eyes, and two heart-shaped spots on the cheeks. His hair was short and was colored white; and he was dressed in the skins of an animal cleverly stitched together." The gigantic man's feet looked huge (actually his feet were covered in animal skin and stuffed with straw to keep them warm), so the Spaniards called him and his people Patagonians, Spanish for "the big-footed people."

The Patagonian danced, sang, and sprinkled sand on his hair. Magellan ordered one of his men to do the same, as a gesture of friendship. The big man drew near. Magellan gave him food, which the man ate voraciously. He swallowed a bucket of water. Then Magellan's men watched in shock as this giant ate two live rats, skin and hair and all. Magellan later captured two Patagonians to bring back to Spain, but they both died onboard the ship. According to Pigafetta, one of the Patagonians died from the heat.

The Discovery

After four months waiting out the storms of winter, Magellan sent one of his five boats south to explore the coast, but the boat was shipwrecked in a squall and one man died. Magellan rescued the remaining men and waited on shore another two months. He could not have known how close he

Ona (also called Selk'nam) hunters in Tierra del Fuego, around the turn of the twentieth century.

It was probably smoke from the fires of the Ona Indians that Magellan first spotted on the north shore of Isla Grande in 1520.

was to finding a safe haven. Further down the coast, only a two-day sail away, was the strait that would bear his name.

On October 8, 1520, the captain gave orders to continue southward. He battled the winds for days, but finally, on October 21, Magellan spotted a cape with cliffs plummeting into the sea. He rounded the cape and entered a big bay of black water. He saw snowcapped mountains in the distance. Everyone on the expedition—except Magellan—thought the bay was a mere fjord, an inlet from the sea that would lead nowhere. The men had explored so many bays and had found so many dead ends with no passage to the Pacific. Why explore this one?

Magellan, however, ordered two of his four ships to travel as far west as they could, but to return within five days. Again the weather turned bad. The wind rose into a gale, then a hurricane. Magellan knew that if his ships were lost, his mission would fail. He could not continue exploring with only two ships left.

After an anxious wait, a lookout from high above on the mast of Magellan's ship spotted a sail, then two sails. The two ships were returning, firing guns and flying flags. They had discovered that the bay kept opening up, through narrows into other bays and farther and farther west, until they knew they had found the passage that Magellan alone had believed existed.

The captain ordered all four ships to head west at once. What a sight that must have been to the natives along shore, to see those four ghostly ships sailing by under a gloomy sky, the first of their kind ever to cross through the strait. Magellan

This illustration from 1594 shows Magellan navigating the strait that would later bear his name. On the right is Patagonia, where a Patagonian giant is swallowing an arrow. On the left is Tierra del Fuego, where the flames represent "the land of fire." An angel seems to guide Magellan through the dangerous waters as Neptune reclines on a cloud.

did not meet the natives, but he saw the smoke from their fires. I imagine it must have been eerie to see that smoke rising from the forests, knowing that somewhere out there people were watching. Who were they?

It must have taken amazing skill in navigation, and perhaps a great deal of luck, too, for Magellan to sail through the treacherous strait. These waters are filled with dangerous shoals and rocks. Wicked squalls come down off the mountains with such force that many future captains and their ships would go under—but not Magellan.

The Portuguese captain spent a month exploring this passage to the other ocean. Finally one of his ships discovered the outlet of the strait into the Pacific. Magellan was a stern and unemotional man, but when he saw the Pacific Ocean, he began to cry, his cheeks wet with tears of joy. He alone had accomplished what so many explorers had only dreamed of doing. He had found a way to sail through the continent; he had found the fabled passage that yoked the Atlantic and Pacific Oceans.

The glory of his discovery, however, was undercut by tragedy. Magellan himself never returned to Spain or to his native Portugal. He died in the Philippines. Of his five ships that left Seville in 1519, only one returned. In September 1522, three years after departure, that lone ship sailed upriver to Seville. Onboard, only eighteen crew members remained from the expedition's original 265. But the first circumnavigation of the globe was complete.

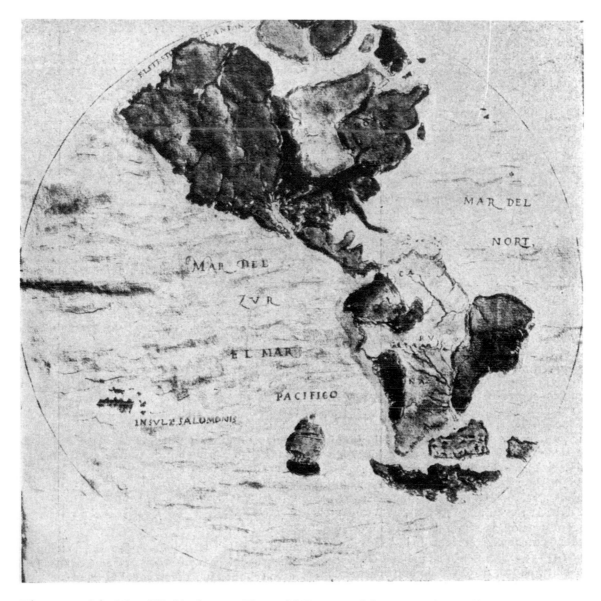

This map of the New World, showing Tierra del Fuego and the Strait of Magellan at the bottom, was drawn around 1568, less than fifty years after Magellan's expedition returned to Spain.

Some local boys spoke to me about their lives in Punta Arenas.

Joshua Slocum: The first man to sail around the world alone.

Joshua Slocum

Punta Arenas, which means "sandy point" in Spanish, was a good place for ships to stop along the Strait of Magellan. It had a protected harbor and lots of fresh water and wood for building and mending ships. Wool and mutton industries in Patagonia developed in the late nineteenth century, and until the Panama Canal was built in 1914, there were many ships stopping in Punta Arenas. Today, the industries here are petroleum and tourism. Modern Punta Arenas owes its beginnings to the California Gold Rush of the 1840s. Prospectors trying to get to California from the east coast of America came around South America to avoid a long and dangerous cross-continental trip. This busy traffic from the forty-niners led to a boom at Punta Arenas, and many of the old buildings from the 1800s still stand in the downtown area.

Riding my bike around the city, I met some local boys. Alberto, Roberto, and Francisco asked me where I was from. They wanted to see a real dollar bill from the United States of America, which I showed them. These kids were like my own kids: they rode scooters, they joked and laughed and teased each other. They said that I should tell the children of North America that the air is good in Punta Arenas and it is a good place to grow up.

One reason I'd come to the end of the earth was to see the place so well described by a great sailor named Joshua Slocum, the author of a wonderful book called *Sailing Alone Around the World*. In 1898, Slocum found out just how treacherous the

"I studied with diligence Neptune's laws, and these laws I tried to obey when I sailed overseas; it was worth the while."

— Joshua Slocum

Strait of Magellan was. He had great difficulty maneuvering his 40-foot boat, the *Spray*, up the strait into the Pacific. It took him two months of fighting wild headwinds and bad weather. Slocum wrote in his log, "In the Strait of Magellan, the greatest vigilance was necessary . . . the greatest danger of the whole voyage . . . "

After being battered by squalls and gales and williwaws (sudden gusts of cold air coming down off the mountains), Slocum had to deal with attacking pirates, too. Of his time in Tierra del Fuego, he wrote, "It was the greatest sea adventure of my life. God knows how my vessel escaped."

Slocum had been warned in Punta Arenas by a Chilean naval officer to hire a crew and to fight the marauders who might attack him in the strait. There was one bad man in particular to watch out for, named Pedro. Shoot first, he was advised. Slocum did nothing of the sort, but he did take an Austrian sailor's advice and bought a load of carpet tacks. He was wise to do so. Those tacks would come in handy, as he was to find out.

Leaving Punta Arenas and heading west toward the Pacific Ocean, Slocum was besieged by the pirates. Several canoes came toward Slocum's boat. He did not want to let the pirates know he was alone, so he made a mannequin out of clothes and set it standing in the front of the *Spray*. He also entered his cabin a few times, quickly changed clothes, and came out the other side dressed differently, hoping to fool the pirates into thinking there were at least three people aboard. I can just picture the desperate sailor changing clothes at breakneck speed in order to save his life.

Slocum on the bow of his legendary boat, the Spray.

On the shores of the Strait of Magellan.

When the canoes came toward him, one man yelled out "Yammerschooner," which was the word the pirates used to demand goods and money. Slocum was forced to take aim and shoot near the lead boat until the pirates turned back to shore.

I shudder to think what Joshua Slocum must have faced on his long voyage. Sailing alone, he piloted his small boat through monstrous waves and devilish currents for months on end. I could imagine myself losing patience in his place and perhaps just giving up.

Weeks passed, and still Slocum could not sail clear into the Pacific. Many times he was forced to find shelter in the lee of an island or a mainland cove, which he found stark and forlorn. On one hill he spotted a pile of rocks, showing that some unknown person had been there. "But how could one tell but that he had died of loneliness and grief?" Slocum wrote.

Now inside the safety of the strait again, exhausted from fighting the sea, Slocum prepared to go to sleep in his cabin. But not before he sprinkled tacks on the deck. They were his first line of defense against the pirate Pedro. Sure enough, Slocum awakened at midnight to the sound of men howling. He rushed onto the deck to see the barefooted Pedro and his men jumping overboard and scrambling into their canoes.

Finally, months after his first attempt, Slocum was able to sail west into the Pacific.

"On February 1 the Spray rounded Cape Virgins and entered the Strait of Magellan. The scene was again real and gloomy; the wind, northeast, and blowing a gale, sent feather-white spume along the coast . . . and the wreck of a great steamship smashed on the beach . . . gave a gloomy aspect to the scene."

— from Sailing Alone Around the World

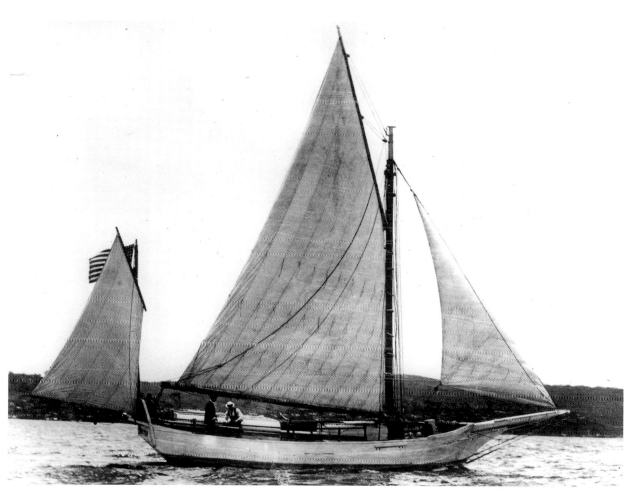

The Spray in full sail.

TWO

Ushuaia, Argentina

The island of Tierra del Fuego is cut in half by the border between Chile and Argentina. I flew over the border on a Twin Otter. My flight from Punta Arenas, Chile, to Ushuaia, Argentina, was like riding a bucking bronco. Snow collected on the wings, tires, and struts of our small plane. We twenty passengers bounced around for an hour through thick clouds, until suddenly we popped out of the brooding skies just over the Beagle Channel, in sight of the most dramatic mountains I have ever seen. Ushuaia is a jewel of a city with its pastel-colored houses and stores, all laid out on the thin strip of land between the snow-clad Andes and the Beagle Channel.

Ushuaia.

The calm waters of Ushuaia harbor.

When the plane was safely on the ground, the Chilean pilot smiled as he pulled a yard-long chunk of ice off the windshield and into the cockpit. The weather in Ushuaia was moody. Just when it seemed like the sun would appear, clouds suddenly descended from the mountains, hail shot from the sky, and the temperature plummeted from a pleasant summer fifty-five degrees fahrenheit to below freezing. The wind started to whip out of the southwest like a screaming banshee.

I had expected to find a desolate and rugged little town at the end of the world. Instead, I discovered that Ushuaia had grown to a city of 45,000. In fact, many tourists come here to embark on research vessels to the Falkland Islands and to Antarctica. Boats of all kinds fill the harbor. Although some old tugboat wrecks tilt in the shallows, the harbor is protected, so it's often calm even while the water in the channel rages.

Here at last was one of the places I had always dreamed of visiting: Ushuaia, the southernmost city in the world. I was so far south on the planet that in January the sun was rising at 4 A.M. and didn't set until 10 P.M.

Ushuaia was the first town settled in Tierra del Fuego. White settlers put down roots on Tierra del Fuego's Isla Grande in 1871. They constructed corrugated iron houses that could withstand the harsh weather conditions. In the early days of European homesteading in Ushuaia, four tribes still lived in the region: the Yámana (also called Yahgan), the Haush, the Alacaluf, and the Ona (or Selk'nam). I had hoped to meet descendants of these Indians, but sadly the tribes had disappeared long ago.

Early settlers began to arrive on the island in the late nineteenth century.

This photograph, which may date from the turn of the twentieth century, shows Ushuaia when it was a small outpost at the end of the earth.

I was surprised at how recently the area had been settled. After Magellan passed through the strait in 1520, others from Europe came through, but no one stopped for long. And there was little contact with the four tribes, who went about living the way they had for thousands of years. Once Ushuaia was settled in the late nineteenth century, however, the Yámana, who lived on the many islands of the archipelago, did not survive long after continued contact with the outsiders.

"The surf was breaking fearfully on the coast, and the spray was carried over a cliff estimated to 200 feet in height . . . At noon a great sea broke over us and filled one of the whale boats, which was obliged to be instantly cut away. The poor Beagle trembled at the shock, and for a few minutes would not obey her helm; but soon, like a good ship that she was, she righted and came up to the wind again."

— from The Voyage of the Beagle

The Beagle.

Yámana

Yámana was what the world's southernmost tribe called themselves, meaning "human" or, simply, just "people." For centuries the area received sporadic yearly visits from sailing ships. One of those ships was the *Beagle*, for which the Beagle Channel was named. The *Beagle*, under the command of Captain Robert Fitzroy, first sailed through the channel in 1829. On the *Beagle's* second voyage in 1832, the legendary scientist Charles Darwin was on board.

Charles Darwin.

Fuegia Basket.

Jemmy Button.

Fuegia Basket and Jemmy Botton were among the Fuegians who were brought to England.

It was on Fitzroy's first voyage that he took four Yámana Indians from the area and carried them back to England with the idea of educating them. He planned to return the Yámana to their native Tierra del Fuego and thereby hoped to introduce Christianity to the tribe. When Darwin sailed into the Channel, three of the native converts were aboard. Darwin watched as the Fuegians were dropped on an island across the channel from Ushuaia. Within weeks, two of the three had taken off their British clothes and returned to their native ways.

Charles Darwin writes in his journal about meeting the Yámana for the first time: "A group of Fuegians, partly concealed by the

entangled forest, were perched on a wild point overhanging the sea; and as we passed by, they sprang up and waving their tattered cloaks sent forth a loud and sonorous shout."

Between 1886 and the early 1900s, a few gold miners came to Tierra del Fuego to get rich. With them came diseases that killed the Indians, who had no natural immunity to the common cold, tuberculosis, and other sicknesses brought by the outsiders. In 1860 there were an estimated 2,500 Yámana. By 1893 there were only 300. A few years later, the tribe was extinct.

The only way I could get a sense of the Indians who had lived in this area was to go to a museum called El Museo del Fin del Mundo, or the Museum at the End of the World. I learned here that the Yámana had dressed in few clothes despite the harsh, cold, and windy environment. Fire was as precious to the Yámana as water is to the Bushmen of the Kalahari. They depended so entirely on the warmth of their fires that they kept them going day and night. Pyrite was struck against a piece of flint to produce sparks, which caught in moss or the down of birds. Most Yámana activities took place near a fire.

The Yámana were nomads, hunters and gatherers living no more than a few days in any one place. They constructed temporary wood huts, or wigwams, one family per dwelling. These were made from interlaced branches with a covering of grass, pieces of bark, and hides. The fire inside the huts never went out. When the hut was abandoned and a family moved on, it could be used by anyone who passed by.

The Yámana lived on a diet of seafood and fowl. They hunted

Native peoples such as the Yámana lived on Tierra del Fuego for over six thousand years.

The native people of Tierra del Fuego never extinguished their fires. Even in this Yámana bark canoe the fire is burning for warmth.

with snares and slings. At night, with the aid of a torch, they caught birds with their bare hands. Penguins and big birds called cormorants were among their favorites. Mussels were their most important source of nutrition because they were easy to find and available year round.

The Yámana used canoes to gather food from the sea. Each family had its own canoe. The Yámana woman usually steered while the man stood on the bow to harpoon a seal.

The tribe often worked together. Whenever a whale was stranded on the beach, all the families came to build a large bonfire, and everyone shared in the blubber.

The increasing presence of settlers in Tierra del Fuego spelled doom for the Yámana and other Indians. Unfortunately, when the sheep farmers came to this land, they killed the llama-like animal called the guanaco, on which the Indians depended for food and clothing. When the guanaco became scarce, the Indians killed the settlers' sheep to try to survive. Some of the sheep farmers started killing the Indians. This was a tragic period in the island's history.

THREE

The Beagle Channel

In Ushuaia, I loved to wake to see new boats arrive in the harbor: navy ships, container boats, tour boats. Every day, when the sun first peeked over the mountains, boats had either arrived or departed. For an entire week, a very rusty, spooky-looking ship called the *Tai An* sat in port.

At 9 P.M., with the summer sun still up in the sky, I rode down to the water. I asked the sailors on the *Tai An* where they were from. They responded in a mixture of Spanish and English that they came from China and were headed to the Falkland Islands.

The next day, from the port, I took a small boat up the Beagle Channel. The water was a gray blue, and I noticed on

South American fur seals.

Tugboat stranded in Ushuaia harbor.

This Chinese sailor was headed for the Falkland Islands.

the charts that the border between Chile and Argentina runs right through the middle of the Channel. Oystercatchers, grebes, steamer ducks, terns, and gulls floated on the water and soared above the big waves. Victor, our captain, told me harrowing stories of shipwrecks in the area. The tug tilting in the harbor, he said, had tried to help raise another wreck when the tug itself had to be abandoned in a storm in the 1950s.

There was a strong smell of rotting fish and kelp as we approached the islands where hundreds of cormorants roosted. Then we came to Isla de los Lobos, with its South American Fur Seals. This is one of the few breeding sites left in Tierra del Fuego for these magnificent creatures. The seals, most of them female, were taking a nap. They lay about indolently as I snapped their photos. And I wondered if Darwin had seen similar animals on this same tiny island as he passed by.

We motored past another island where mustard-colored lichen covered the rocks. Pieces of a wreck were scattered about the shore. Here, too, was the southernmost lighthouse in the world, a stark exclamation point above a forlorn wreckage.

Late in the afternoon, I stepped out of the boat onto Bridges Island and noticed the delicacy and beauty of the flora, so bright against the gray land. I saw *calafate*, a yellow flower on a thorny bush, and firebrush, which the Yámana called *muhgua*. *Murtilla* are the little red berries we call mountain berry, and a big bulbous green plant, the "balsam bog," is a plant from which the Yámana ate the roots. I saw evidence of the Yámana people, too. Victor pointed to small circular depressions in the earth where native wigwams had sat more than a hundred years before.

Cormorants.

31

An Ona Indian hut or wigwam.

The southernmost lighthouse in the world in the Beagle Channel.

It felt good to stretch my legs. As I walked, I imagined myself following in the footsteps of the great naturalist Charles Darwin. During his explorations on the *Beagle* he made detailed observations of this starkly beautiful land. He also made forays into the interior. He climbed mountains and explored the coasts, and he found the interior of the island peculiarly unproductive. He found few mammals other than the mouse, the fox, a bat, the sea otter, and the guanaco. He found no reptiles, and few beetles. He found very few butterflies and bees, and no crickets. But on the coast, he found kelp, large algae teeming

The Beagle Channel viewed from the shores of Bridges Island.

Bridges Island: The vegetation is colorful and the kelp (bottom photo) is abundant.

with fish and mollusks, and all the many creatures that the coastal penguins, seals, and birds needed to thrive. He imagined that if the kelp were destroyed, the creatures that the Yámana ate would disappear and so would the Yámana.

Cape San Pablo

Early one morning I rode north to Cape San Pablo on the Atlantic coast of Isla Grande. I climbed over the Garibaldi Pass, winding and twisting on loose gravel, and passed lovely glacial lakes high in the mountains. Then I came down on the

Curious guanaco.

Picturesque sheep farms are a common sight in Patagonia.

north side of the Andes into the central region of the island. Here the flat plains of the pampas were dotted with sheep farms raked by relentless winds.

To reach San Pablo, I took a turn off the main road onto a dirt road. There had been a lot of rain, so the wheel ruts were full of water. I traveled a few miles up the road past low beech forests covered in dangling light green lichen, when suddenly I spotted a big creature staring at me from a nearby forest. I grabbed my camera, but before I could photograph the wild guanaco, cousin of the llama, the creature had walked timidly behind a tree. As I stood in that silence, a whole bunch of the beasts started to laugh at me from behind the trees, a sort of weird chattering barking sound.

The guanaco, often described as elegant, graceful, or noble, is most populous in the mountains and on the eastern peninsula of Tierra del Fuego because few humans come this way. I was lucky to catch sight of these beautiful animals. Once they took a good look at me and satisfied their curiosity, they wandered shyly back into the forest.

I traveled deeper into the interior, past tidy Patagonian sheep farms, with their many white- and red-painted outbuildings and well-maintained corrals. The fields had turned emerald green from all the rain.

As I got closer to the coast and farther away from the farms, the forests contained stunted beech trees with hanging lichen, giving them a primordial and eerie appearance. These forests are filled with dead wood, twisted and rotten at the core.

Patagonian wool and mutton industries began in the late nineteenth century.

Desdemona: *Thousands of ships like this old steamer have foundered off the shores of Tierra del Fuego.*

In one pasture there was a flock of sea birds called black-faced ibis. With hooked beaks and yellow heads, they made odd alarm calls when I got too close. I stalked a large bird of prey called the crested caracara. And high up on a cliff road above the Atlantic Ocean, I surprised another group of guanaco. They were so wild, they were not afraid of me. I caught them lying down. They got up one by one, taking their time. They gazed at me from behind the wind-blown trees like bemused camels.

Far below, the surf of the Atlantic pounded on the beach. As far as the eye could see, there was nothing but open water, no longer hemmed in by the mountains along the Beagle Channel. Finally I'd reached the eastern shore of Tierra del Fuego and the Atlantic, where so many sailors had passed on their way to round the Horn into the Pacific.

When I got to Cape San Pablo at the end of the road, I found an old derelict steamer rusting and tilting in the sand. Victor had told me that his friend's father, who was captain of the *Desdemona*, had been looking at the wrong charts in a violent storm. The *Desdemona* was now just one more wreck among thousands.

Late in the day, the rain clouds swept in from the south and the sun disappeared once again. I reached the end of the road and knew it was time to head back.

FOUR

Harberton

For my last full day in the Ushuaia area, I traveled down the coast of the Beagle Channel to visit the Goodalls, relatives of the first permanent resident of Tierra del Fuego. The family lives at a place called Harberton, which was the first sheep farm established in the Land of Fire.

In 1886, Thomas Bridges, who had worked as a missionary with the Yámana for thirty years, quit the mission and became a farmer. His *estancia*, or farm, is truly gargantuan. It encompasses four mountains, three rivers, numerous lakes and islands and swamps.

The Andes Mountains along the Beagle Channel.

Thomas Bridges, founder of Harberton, was initiated into the Yámana tribe.

(right) *Anne, a descendant of Thomas Bridges, with her daughter Selina.*

I arrived at Harberton on a sunny day and instantly fell in love with the estancia, which is comprised of the main farmhouse, the white outbuildings, the sheep-shearing barn, and a few boats moored in a perfect little harbor facing the Andes. The mountains that rise 4,700 feet from the sea are like daggers held to the sky.

Harberton even today has no phone. The generator that produces the electricity for the lights sounds like a helicopter cutting up the air. I met Anne Goodall, a descendant of Thomas Bridges. Anne is a cowgirl, tough and gutsy. She grew up riding with her dad on the farm, herding the sheep. Now she is her father's righthand person for maintaining the farm.

Anne speaks English with a slight Spanish accent. She

Cattle ranch near Harberton.

explained that they raised mostly cattle today and not sheep. She herds, she brands, and she moves the cattle from one grazing spot to another. Often Anne will ride with her thirteen-year-old daughter, just the way her father rode with her when she was a young girl.

Anne invited me to go along with her three daughters and some friends out to Penguin Island, to visit the Magellan penguins. I was delighted to see how innocent and happy this family was, as they played in the natural world. Even the kids did not seem to need all

Penguin Island.

the computers and conveniences of our modern civilization. Many species of birds and the playful penguins amused them for hours. Shouts of joy rose from the boat when someone spotted albatrosses swirling high overhead under the clouds.

When we got back to the estancia, we drank *maté* together, a strong Argentine tea served in a round gourd and sipped through a silver straw. I liked the bitter taste of the tea. I thanked them all for including me on one of their family trips into the Channel.

On my back to Ushuaia, the weather changed dramatically. It started to hail. Ice pellets shot from an angry sky, and I was reminded that I was very near Cape Horn at the bottom of the world, and only hundreds of miles from Antarctica.

The Goodalls and friends.

EPILOGUE

Before flying back home to the United States, I stopped again in Punta Arenas. I rode my bike to end of the road, the last place you can ride on the continent, and found a little fishing village called Bahia Mesna. Near the water, a fisherman was filleting a fish for some friends. He had a mischievous gleam in his eyes, and I thought he could be a descendant of that marauder Pedro who had given Slocum such trouble in the Strait of Magellan.

On the road leading from the village, I discovered the forlorn grave site of Commander Pringle Stokes of the HMS *Beagle*, who died here while surveying Tierra del Fuego on the *Beagle*'s first journey. In the rain, the grave seemed almost pitiful in this

Fishing boats in the harbor of Bahia Mesna.

The grave site of Commander Stokes of the HMS Beagle, who died in 1828 "from the effects of the anxieties and hardships incurred while surveying the western shores of Tierra del Fuego."

lonely spot. Then I found a barren promontory known as Puerto Hambre, Port Famine. In the late sixteenth century, a few Spaniards had tried to establish a colony here but had all died of hunger.

Darwin came to Port Famine for his third and final time at the beginning of the winter of 1834. The Yámana he encountered were a sorry sight. He described the Indians as survivors of rain, hail, snow, and sleet, living only on mussels and berries, their tattered clothes burned from sleeping so close to the fire.

Darwin's parting glance at the region evoked images of terror. When the great naturalist looked into the wild waters at the end of the earth, he brooded: "One sight of such a coast is enough to make a landsman dream for a week about shipwrecks, peril, and death, and with this sight we bade farewell forever to Tierra del Fuego."

For me, too, it was time to go. But I would leave much happier than Darwin.

I rode down to the beach and sat on the Strait of Magellan, looking across at Isla Grande, at the big boats coming and going, and at the busy petrels, gulls, and ducks.

It was icy cold and blowing whitecaps out beyond the lee of the land. All about me were glaciers and snowcapped mountains, desolation and breathtaking beauty. Magellan passed by nearly five hundred years ago, the first European sailor to spy this windswept place. And still Tierra del Fuego is a land of adventure and dreams.

ARTE DE LA
VERDADERA NA-
VEGACION.

En que se trata de la machina del mũdo, es a faber, Cielos, y Elementos: de las mareas, y señales de tẽpestades: del Aguja de marear: del modo de hazer cartas de nauegar: del vso dellas: de la declinacion y rodeo, que comunmente hazenlos pilotos: del modo verdadero de nauegar por circulo menor: por linea recta sin declinacion ni rodeo: el modo como se sabra el camino, y leguas que ha nauegado el piloto, por qualquier ruinbo: y vltimamente el saber tomar el altura del Polo.

DIRIGIDA A LA S.C.R.M. DEL REY DON Phelippe el tercero, señor nuestro.

COMPVESTA POR PEDRO DE SYRIA, NATVRAL de la ciudad de Valencia, y Letrado en la dicha ciudad.

CON PRIVILEGIO

Impressa en Valencia, en casa de Iuan Chrysostomo Garriz, junto al molino de Rouella. Año 1602.

Further Reading

For further reading, I suggest the following books for young readers:

Fritz, Jean. *Around the World in a Hundred Years: From Henry the Navigator to Magellan.* Putnam & Grosset, 1994.

Fullick, Ann. *Charles Darwin,* (Groundbreakers). Heinemann Library, 2000.

Gallagher, Jim. *Ferdinand Magellan and the First Voyage Around the World,* (Explorers of New Worlds series). Chelsea House, 2000.

The original writings of the explorers themselves are extremely interesting. To learn more about Ferdinand Magellan, see *Magellan's Voyage: A Narrative Account of the First Circumnavigation* by Antonio Pigafetta, New York: Dover Publications, 1994. Antonio Pigafetta sailed with Magellan, and his journals provide a wonderful firsthand account of the great voyage.

To read about Joshua Slocum's adventures, see the classic book *Sailing Alone Around the World* by Joshua Slocum, New York: Penguin, 1999.

And for Charles Darwin's own observations, take a look at Chapter Ten, entitled "Tierra del Fuego," in *The Voyage of the* Beagle: *Darwin's Five-Year Circumnavigation*, Narrative Press, 2001.

INDEX